W9-AWW-036

SPACE

HOW TO USE YOUR SD-X READER WITH THIS BOOK

This highly interactive book lets you explore American biographies in an interactive format. You can read the book and study the photographs and illustrations, but a touch of the SD-X Reader adds in-depth audio information, word definitions, and learning games to the page.

1. Press the Power button to turn the SD-X Reader on or off. The LED will light up when the SD-X Reader is on.

2. Touch the volume buttons found on this page or on the Table of Contents page to adjust the volume.

3. Touch photographs and illustrations to hear additional information. Page headers and words or phrases that are in a different size or color than the surrounding text often provide a definition or more information.

4. As you explore the page, you'll encounter games and quizzes. Touch the text or image that started the game to stop playing.

5. After two minutes of inactivity, the Reader will beep and go to sleep.

6. If the batteries are low, the Reader will beep twice and the LED will start blinking. Replace the batteries by following the instructions on the next page. The SD-X Reader uses two AAA batteries.

7. To use headphones or earbuds, plug them into the headphone jack on the bottom of the SD-X Reader.

CHANGE THE VOLUME WITH THESE BUTTONS

▲ ▼
UP   DOWN

Battery Information
Interactive Pen includes 2 replaceable AAA batteries (UM-4 or LR03).

Battery Installation
1. Open battery door with small flat-head or Phillips screwdriver.
2. Install new batteries according to +/- polarity. If batteries are not installed properly, the device will not function.
3. Replace battery door; secure with small screw.

Battery Safety
Batteries must be replaced by adults only. Properly dispose of used batteries. Do not dispose of batteries in fire; batteries may explode or leak. See battery manufacturer for disposal recommendations. Do not mix alkaline, standard (carbon-zinc), or rechargeable (nickel-cadmium) batteries. Do not mix old and new batteries. Only recommended batteries of the same or equivalent type should be used. Remove weakened or dead batteries. Never short-circuit the supply terminals. Non-rechargeable batteries are not to be recharged. Do not use rechargeable batteries. If batteries are swallowed, in the USA, promptly see a doctor and have the doctor phone 1-202-625-3333 collect. In other countries, have the doctor call your local poison control center. Batteries should be changed when sounds mix, distort, or become otherwise unintelligible as batteries weaken. The electrostatic discharge may interfere with the sound module. If this occurs, please simply restart the product.

In Europe, the dustbin symbol indicates that batteries, rechargeable batteries, button cells, battery packs, and similar materials must not be discarded in household waste. Batteries containing hazardous substances are harmful to the environment and to health. Please help to protect the environment from health risks by telling your children to dispose of batteries properly and by taking batteries to local collection points. Batteries handled in this manner are safely recycled.

Warning: Changes or modifications to this unit not expressly approved by the party responsible for compliance could void the user's authority to operate the equipment.

NOTE: This equipment has been tested and found to comply with the limits for a Class B digital device, pursuant to Part 15 of the FCC Rules. These limits are designed to provide reasonable protection against harmful interference in a residential installation. This equipment generates, uses, and can radiate radio frequency energy and, if not installed and used in accordance with the instructions, may cause harmful interference to radio communications. However, there is no guarantee that interference will not occur in a particular installation. If this equipment does cause harmful interference to radio or television reception, which can be determined by turning the equipment off and on, the user is encouraged to try to correct the interference by one or more of the following measures: Reorient or relocate the receiving antenna. Increase the separation between the equipment and receiver. Connect the equipment into an outlet on a circuit different from that to which the receiver is connected. Consult the dealer or an experienced radio TV technician for help.

Cover art: Shutterstock.com; Smithsonian Institution
Interior art: NASA; Shutterstock.com; Smithsonian Institution
© 2016 Publications International, Ltd. All rights reserved.
The Smithsonian name and logo are registered trademarks of the Smithsonian Institution.
SD-X Interactive is a registered trademark in the United States and Canada.
Product and sound element design, engineering, and reproduction are proprietary technologies of Publications International, Ltd.

This publication may not be reproduced or quoted from in whole or in part by any means whatsoever without written permission from:

Louis Weber, CEO
Publications International, Ltd.
8140 Lehigh Avenue
Morton Grove, IL 60053

Permission is never granted for commercial purposes.

 Publications International, Ltd.

Customer service:
customer_service@pubint.com

ISBN: 978-1-68022-384-2

Manufactured in China.

8 7 6 5 4 3 2 1

CONTENTS

CHANGE THE VOLUME WITH THESE BUTTONS

UP   DOWN

INTRODUCTION

The National Air and Space Museum displays objects from its collections at the Museum in Washington, DC and the Steven F. Udvar-Hazy Center in Chantilly, VA. It is the largest of 19 museums included in the Smithsonian Institution. It welcomes on average eight million people annually, making it the most visited museum complex in the country. The Museum's collection includes objects, artwork, archival photographs, documents, and more. This book explores some of the topics and information found at the Museum.

A PLACE FOR SPACE

ON DISPLAY

MISSION: COMMEMORATE, EDUCATE, INSPIRE

The Museum is best known for its rare and historically significant aircraft and spacecraft. The object collection also includes engines, instruments, equipment, models, artwork, spacesuits, and much more. Altogether, the collection includes more than 30,000 aviation and 9,000 space objects. About 20 percent of the collection, including about 80 percent of the largest aircraft and spacecraft are on public display.

GOES SATELLITE

VOYAGER SPACECRAFT MOCK-UP, FULL SCALE

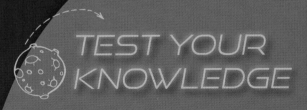

TEST YOUR KNOWLEDGE

PLANETARIUM

OBSERVATORY

EXHIBITION

MUSEUM

A BIG BEGINNING

Everywhere we look in the distant regions of space, galaxies appear to be rushing away from us at faster and faster speeds. But the galaxies are not really moving. The space between the galaxies is stretching.

The Big Bang wasn't a massive explosion with matter and energy flying off into a previously empty space. Instead, imagine the entire universe as a giant expanding bubble with the galaxies floating on its surface. The growing surface moves the galaxies apart, but the individual galaxies, stars and planets stay the same size.

HOW DO WE DEFINE DISTANCE IN SPACE?

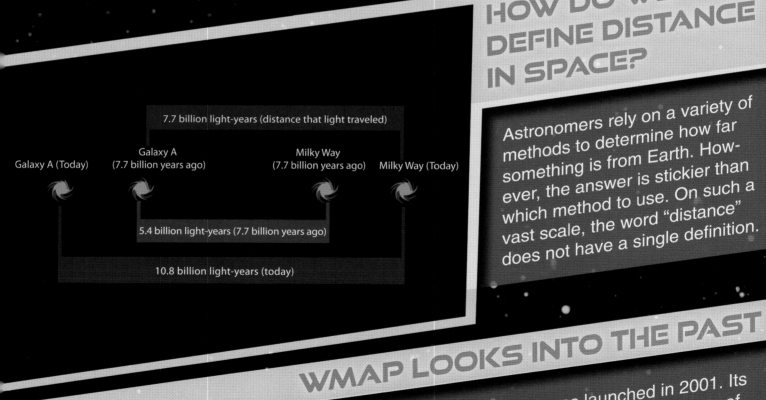

7.7 billion light-years (distance that light traveled)

Galaxy A (Today)

Galaxy A (7.7 billion years ago)

Milky Way (7.7 billion years ago)

Milky Way (Today)

5.4 billion light-years (7.7 billion years ago)

10.8 billion light-years (today)

Astronomers rely on a variety of methods to determine how far something is from Earth. However, the answer is stickier than which method to use. On such a vast scale, the word "distance" does not have a single definition.

WMAP LOOKS INTO THE PAST

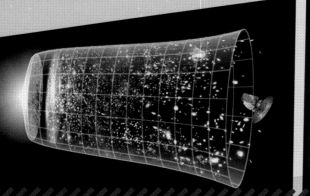

NASA's WMAP spacecraft was launched in 2001. Its observations helped scientists determine the age of the universe. This model shows the evolution of the universe over 13.77 billion years. The far left depicts the earliest moment we can now probe, when a period of "inflation" produced a burst of exponential growth in the universe.

HUBBLE ULTRA DEEP FIELD

ARE THERE OTHER UNIVERSES ?

Touch one of the dates below to learn how scientists have refined their ideas over time.

1900 – 1949

1950 – 1989

1990 – 1999

2000s

HOW DID THE UNIVERSE BEGIN?

Standard theory holds that the universe began about 13.7 billion years ago. After a brief period of extremely rapid expansion, the universe continued to expand at a slower rate, allowing matter to condense and form into clumps of stars, which later developed into galaxies.

Determining the age of the universe reached a crisis in 1994 when astronomers estimated an age of 11 billion years. This conflicted with the age of globular clusters, which had been dated as 12 to 15 billion years old. New techniques have enabled astronomers to specify the age of the universe with more certainty. Further refining of the universe's age become possible in 2003 when NASA's WMAP satellite provided an extremely detailed picture of minor temperature fluctuations in the fading afterglow of radiation from the Big Bang.

1000 BLACK HOLES

BLACK HOLES
TRUE OR FALSE

TRUE

FALSE

A UNIVERSE OF GALAXIES

Soon after the Big Bang, the universe evolved from a hot primordial plasma, which we now observe as the cosmic microwave background (CMB), to a space filled with dark matter, radiation, and neutral gas. During recombination, the universe entered a starless dark age. Over the next several hundred million years, gravity produced a web of cores and interconnecting filamentary structure. As the cores grew, portions collapsed to form the first stars and clusters of stars. Eventually, groups of star clusters surrounded by gas became the first galaxies.

LARGE MAGELLANIC CLOUD

ANDROMEDA GALAXY

TRIANGULUM GALAXY

CENTAURUS A GALAXY

GALAXY NGC 6240

THE ANTENNAE

GALAXY THEORIES OVER TIME

1900-1949

1950-1989

1990-1999

2000

OUR GALAXY

The Milky Way Galaxy is 100,000 **LIGHT-YEARS** across and contains 200 to 400 billion stars. Galaxies began to take shape soon after the birth of the universe, and gravity holds them together.

MILKY WAY CENTER

A VIEW OF OUR GALAXY FROM ABOVE . . .

YOU ARE HERE

MILKY WAY
TRUE OR FALSE

TRUE

FALSE

PEELING BACK THE LAYERS

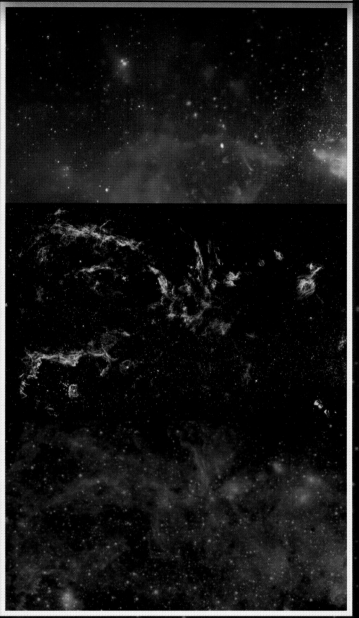

GALACTIC STRUCTURE

While our optical view of the Milky Way is limited by interstellar dust to just a small fraction of the distance across the galactic disk, at radio wavelengths emissions from interstellar gas in its various forms can be readily observed throughout the galaxy. For this reason, radio astronomers have played a leading role in galactic structure research since the 1950s, when the first large-scale surveys of interstellar atomic hydrogen were carried out.

We now have a fairly uniform survey of the entire molecular galaxy. This survey is widely used by galactic astronomers and continues to yield new results on star formation and galactic structure, including the recent discovery of two new spiral arm features.

. . . AND FROM THE SIDE

NUCLEAR
BULGE

GALACTIC
DISK

SUN

GLOBULAR
CLUSTER

HALO

A STAR IS BORN

Our Sun is only one of 100 billion stars in our galaxy. Without it, life on Earth would not be possible. What we know about our Sun serves as the foundation for what we understand about distant stars.

SPECTRUM OF THE SUN

When the light from our Sun passes through a **SPECTROSCOPE**, the light waves are separated into a spectrum of colors with dark, vertical lines throughout. Each chemical element absorbs certain wavelengths of light represented by the dark lines and emits others represented by the colors.

LIGHT OF ALL KINDS

CLOSE-UPS FROM TRACE

Object:
Solar Flares

Distance from Earth:
8.3 light-minutes

Size:
100,000–400,000 km
(62,000–248,000 mi)

Telescope:
Transition Region and
Coronal Explorer (TRACE)

Light:
Ultraviolet (various wavelengths)

HOW DO WE KNOW ABOUT OUR SUN'S EARLY HISTORY?

We can't go back in time to watch our Sun's birth, but meteorites found on Earth provide clues to its past.

The Allende Meteorite, which fell in Mexico in 1969, contains clumps of dust grains formed very near the infant Sun. But the Allende Meteorite came from the asteroid belt, which is farther from the Sun than Earth.

How did the dust get there? A protostar (a star whose core has not yet started fusing hydrogen atoms into helium) rotates very quickly, spewing jets of hot matter from its poles. This matter ends up far from where it was formed. Astronomers see this process in faraway star nurseries, such as the Carina Nebula.

LIFE CYCLE OF OUR SUN

STELLAR NEBULA

PROTOSTAR

YELLOW STAR

RED GIANT

PLANETARY NEBULA AND WHITE DWARF

BLACK DWARF

KEEP IT LIGHT

INFRARED

RADIO

X-RAY

VISIBLE

GAMMA RAY

PLANETS

Humans have wondered about the planets for centuries, but it is only in recent decades that spacecraft have revealed detailed views of them. To us they are no longer just specks of light, but worlds dramatically diverse yet bound by common processes that shape their surfaces and environments.

PTOLEMY'S PLANETARY SYSTEM

Systema Ptolemaicum

Fig.

COPERNICUS

COMPARING PLANETARY SURFACE FEATURES

ATMOSPHERES

VOLCANOES

IMPACT FEATURES

WATER AND ICE

WIND

TELESCOPE IN SPACE

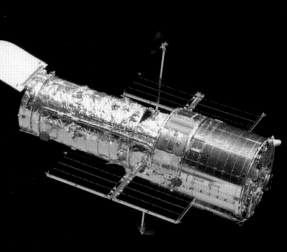

HOW DO PLANETS FORM?

Every planetary system forms in a thin disk of gas and dust orbiting a young star. Small dust grains, a micron or two in size, collide and merge into large aggregates that settle into the midplane of the disk. In the midplane, aggregates grow into planetesimals with diameters of roughly one kilometer. Collisions between planetesimals produce planets.

PLANET MATCH

⊕ ☽ ☉ ☿ ♀ ♂

♃ ⛢ ♄ ♆ ♀ ♇

MERCURY

Mercury may be seen as an evening "star" near where the sun has set, or as a morning "star" near where the sun will rise. The ancient Greeks called the evening star Hermes and the morning star Apollo, believing them to be different objects. The planet is named for Mercury, the Roman messenger of the gods.

Mean distance from Sun: 0.3871 <u>AU</u> (57,910,000 km/35,980,000 mi)
Diameter: 4,878 km (3,031 mi)
Length of year: 88 days
Rotation period: 58.65 days
Mean orbital velocity: 48 km/s (30 mi/s)
Inclination of axis: 2°
Average temperature: 800° F (427° C) day
-300° F (-183° C) night

Number of observed satellites: 0

Comparisons with Earth
Mean distance from Sun: 0.387 x Earth's
Diameter: 0.38 x Earth's
Mass: 0.055 x Earth's
Density: Slightly less than Earth's

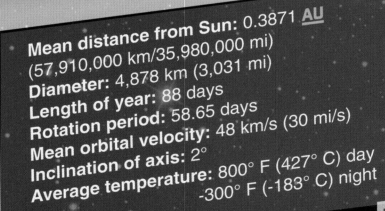

CALORIS IMPACT BASIN

VOLCANISM

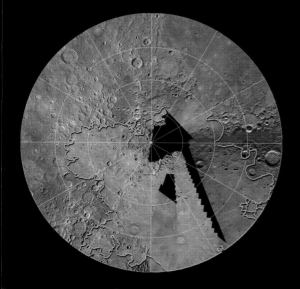

WATER ICE

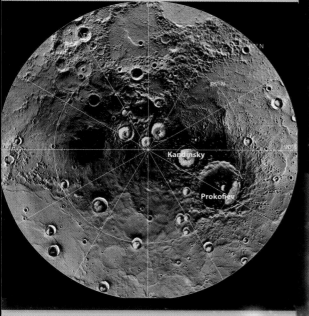

A SHRINKING PLANET?

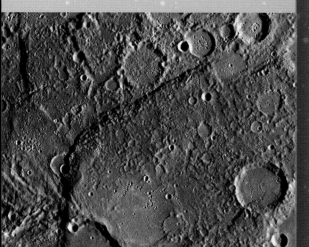

EARTH-BASED OBSERVATIONS OF MERCURY

WHAT DO YOU KNOW ABOUT MERCURY?

FACT
FICTION

IMPORTANT DATES

1965   1991   1975

2011   1631

VENUS

At its closest, Venus is only 42 million kilometers (26 million miles) from Earth. Venus has a thick atmosphere of carbon dioxide. Atmospheric pressure at the surface is 90 times that of Earth. Because Venus is nearer the Sun than Earth and has a very thick atmosphere, the surface temperature is extremely high, as much as 475° Celsius (900° Farenheit).

Mean distance from Sun: 0.7233 AU (108,200,000 km/67,230,000 mi)
Diameter: 12,102 km (7,520 mi)
Length of year: 225 days
Rotation period: 243 days (RETROGRADE)
Mean orbital velocity: 35 km/sec (21.8 mi/sec)
Inclination of axis: 177.3°
Number of observed satellites: 0

Comparisons with Earth
Mean distance from Sun: 0.723 x Earth's
Diameter: 0.95 x Earth's
Mass: 0.81 x Earth's
Density: 0.9 x Earth's

CORONAE

GREAT VOLCANOES

DRY, HOT, AND DEADLY

Sometime in its history, Venus underwent a catastrophic "runaway greenhouse" process: the dense carbon dioxide atmosphere trapped heat from the Sun and raised the surface temperature to 475°C (900°F). Any water that existed boiled away; only trace amounts remain. The upper atmosphere contains layers of clouds and hazes, most of which consist of droplets of sulfuric acid.

CRATERS ON VENUS

SEEING THROUGH THE CLOUDS

WHAT DO YOU KNOW ABOUT VENUS?

FACT

FICTION

EARTH

The Earth and its environment may be divided into several realms, the names of which end in -sphere. These spheres include the ATMOSPHERE (air), LITHOSPHERE (rocks), the HYDROSPHERE (water), and the MAGNETOSPHERE (magnetic fields).

Mean distance from Sun: 1 AU (149,600,000 km/ 92,960,000 mi)
Diameter: 12,756 km (7,926 mi)
Length of year: 365.26 days
Rotation period: 23.93 hours

Mean orbital velocity: 29.79 km/ sec (18.6 mi/sec)
Inclination of axis: 23.45°
Average temperature: 59° F (15° C)
Number of observed satellites: 1

EXPLORER 1

THE SHAPE OF THE EARTH

EXPLORING EARTH FROM ORBIT

The Earth, like other planets, is explored by spacecraft. Earth-orbiting spacecraft observe phenomena that are large and global in scale. Using a variety of sensors, satellites may record data that would require tens of thousands of ground-based measurements. Much has been learned about our planet from the vantage point of space that we could not see from the ground.

AURORAE

SIMILAR YET DIFFERENT

CRATER

MOON

CLOUDS

ICE

WIND

OUR MOON

A mere 386,000 kilometers (240,000 miles) away, the Moon is our closest neighbor. From lunar rocks, we have learned that this body's amazing origins are intimately linked to the Earth's. Yet, the Moon bears little resemblance to our own planet. The quiet Moon we see today belies the violence of its distant past.

The Moon's Vital Statistics

Diameter: 3,476 km (2,160 mi)

Atmosphere: With virtually no atmosphere, the Moon has no wind or water to alter its landscape. Also, there is no protection from meteoroids and harsh solar radiation.

Surface: Craters of all sizes dominate the lunar landscape. the pockmarked surface has been shaped by 4.4 billion years of meteoroid bombardment.

Water: The Moon is bone dry.

1. THE BIRTH OF THE MOON

2. MAGMA OCEAN: 4.5–4.4 BILLION YEARS AGO

3. THE BIG BARRAGE: 4–3.9 BILLION YEARS AGO

THE MOON'S NORTH POLE

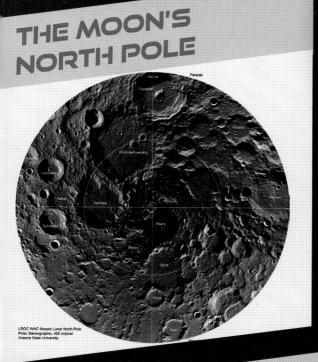

LROC WAC Mosaic Lunar North Pole
Polar Stereographic, 400 m/pixel
Arizona State University

EARTH, SUN, OR MOON?

MOON

SUN

EARTH

MOON GEOLOGY

REGOLITH

BASALT

FELDSPAR

BRECCIA

ANORTHOSITE

YOUNG FAULT SCARPS

GEOLOGIC HISTORY

The Moon's special properties hint that it formed in an unusual way. Compared with other moons and their planets, the Moon is unusually large in relation to its primary body, Earth. Also, the Moon is largely devoid of water and elements with low boiling points—a clue that high temperatures were involved in its formation. Theories about the Moon's origins have been plentiful. But lunar rocks brought back by Apollo astronauts finally provided solid evidence of the Moon's extraordinary history.

4. AGE OF VOLCANISM: 4.2–3.1 BILLION YEARS AGO

5. THE TUMULT WANES: 3.1 BILLION YEARS AGO–NOW

AIMING FOR THE MOON

The space age began on October 4, 1957, when the Soviet Union orbited Sputnik I, the world's first artificial satellite. On November 3, 1957, the Soviets launched Sputnik II. Included in the payload was a dog named Laika, the first living being sent into space. Initial American attempts to meet the Soviet challenge ended in failure, inciting widespread public agitation that the United States was falling behind in this new, crucial arena.

BUILDING A MOON ROCKET

1958: NASA

1959: MONKEYS IN SPACE

1961: THE MOON DECISION

1961–1965: RANGER MISSIONS

1962: ASTRONAUT IN ORBIT

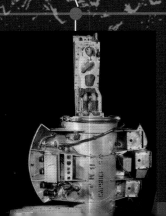

THE FIRST AMERICAN ASTRONAUTS

MISSION ACCOMPLISHMENTS

MERCURY
SURVEYOR
GEMINI
RANGER
APOLLO

Walter M. "Wally" Schirra Jr., Donald K. "Deke" Slayton, John H. Glenn Jr., M. Scott Carpenter, (back row) Alan B. Shepard Jr., Virgil I. "Gus" Grissom and L. Gordon Cooper, Jr.

FIRST AROUND THE MOON

1964: GEMINI MISSIONS

1965: FIRST SPACEWALK

1966–1968: SURVEYOR MISSIONS

1966–1967: LUNAR ORBITER MISSIONS

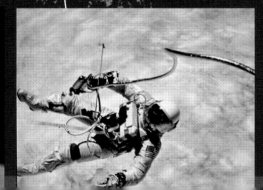

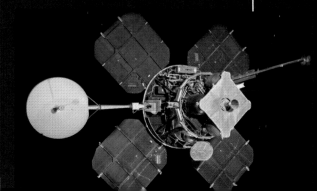

APOLLO TO THE MOON

On July 16 a Saturn V rocket, carrying three astronauts, the Command Module *Columbia*, a Service Module, and the Lunar Module *Eagle*, lifted off. On July 19 Apollo 11 reached lunar orbit and on the 20th Armstrong and Aldrin descended to the surface of the Moon in the Lunar Module, while Collins remained in the orbiting spacecraft. Later that day Armstrong emerged from *Eagle*, descended its ladder, and touched the Moon, offering his famous commemoration of the moment: "one small step for (a) man, one giant leap for mankind."

About 27 hours later, Armstrong and Aldrin guided the ascent stage of their module to a rendezvous with Collins and the orbiting spacecraft. On July 22 Apollo 11 left lunar orbit for the journey back to Earth. *Columbia* and the three astronauts splashed down southwest of Hawaii on the 24th, fulfilling Kennedy's challenge and returning to a tumultuous welcome.

COMMAND MODULE *COLUMBIA*

LUNAR MODULE *EAGLE*

DOING EVA

Astronauts Armstrong and Aldrin completed the first EVA (extra-vehicular activity) on the surface of the moon in July 1969.

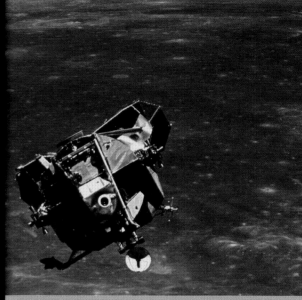

END OF AN ERA

ASCENT FROM THE MOON

Helmet and gloves used in training by Apollo 15 astronaut James Irwin; boots used in Mercury program training by astronaut Gordon Cooper, on display in the James S. McDonnell Space Hangar at the National Air and Space Museum's Steven F. Udvar-Hazy Center.

WHAT IS THAT THING?

LATER MISSIONS

After Apollo 11, NASA sent six more flights to the Moon: Apollo missions 12 through 17. Only Apollo 13 failed to make a lunar landing when an accident en route to the Moon forced the crew to abandon the mission and return to Earth after reaching lunar orbit. The last flight, Apollo 17, occurred in December 1972.

SPACECRAFT AND VEHICLES

Neil Armstrong's first steps on the Moon marked the pinnacle of achievement of the human spaceflight effort through the sixties. But Apollo was only the last step in a series of spaceflight programs, beginning with the single-seat Mercury, followed by the Gemini program where Americans learned to live in orbit, and culminating with Apollo 17, the last human mission to the Moon.

MERCURY CAPSULE

1.5 MILLION POUNDS OF THRUST

Go Baby, Go!

DRIVING ON THE MOON

MOON LANDER

LUNAR MODULE ASCENT ENGINE

GEMINI VII

FIRSTS IN SPACE

JOHN GLENN
(1962)

GORDON COOPER
(1963)

VIRGIL GRISSOM
(1965)

ALAN SHEPARD
(1971)

PAUL WEITZ
(1973)

MARS

Telescopic views suggested to early observers that the climate of Mars changed seasonally. We now know that even greater changes have occurred over billions of years. Great volcanoes have risen. Floodwaters have raced across the surface. Giant impacts have altered the landscape. Today, wind is the only major force of change, but the rocks and soil and landscape still hold clues to the planet's past. Why has Mars changed so much over time? Did life evolve there when conditions were more favorable? Mars continues to challenge each new generation of explorers, and understanding Mars may help us discover our own future in the solar system.

Mean distance from Sun: 1.524 AU (228,000,000 km/141,700,000 mi)
Diameter: 6,792 km (4,220 mi)
Length of year: 687 days
Rotation period: 24 hr 37 min
Mean orbital velocity: 24.14 km/sec (15 mi/sec)
Inclination of axis: 25.2°

Mean density: 3.95 grams/cm°
Inclination to ecliptic: 1.85°
Number of observed satellites: 2

Comparisons with Earth
Average distance from Sun: 1.52 x Earth
Diameter: 0.532 x Earth
Mass: 0.108 x Earth
Density: 0.7 x Earth

LANDSCAPE AND INTERIOR

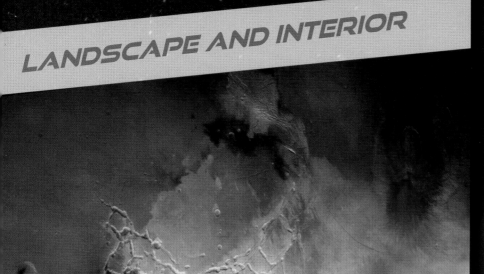

WATER ON MARS

NORTH POLAR CAP

MAJOR LANDFORMS

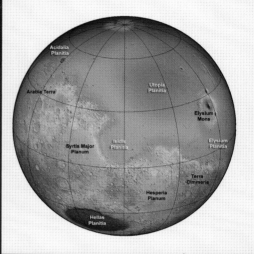

THE MOONS OF MARS

Mars is orbited by two small, potato-shaped satellites, Phobos and Deimos. These tiny Martian satellites are thought to be captured asteroids composed of dark, carbon-rich rock. Each satellite has been heavily cratered by impacting meteoritic debris.

MARS OR EARTH?

MARS

EARTH

EXPLORING THE RED PLANET

Over the past few decades, the robotic spacecraft we've sent to Mars—orbiters, landers, and rovers—have vastly deepened our understanding of the Red Planet. We've come to know Mars not just as an image through a telescope, but also as a unique and intriguing world.

FROM BITS OF DATA TO SCIENCE

To understand Mars, scientists measure many aspects of the surface, atmosphere, and interior. They can make some of these measurements from Earth, but most require spacecraft on or orbiting the planet. Spacecraft instruments measure specific physical properties and are calibrated to match the results of other devices that observe the same conditions. The actual measurements are made by a computer, which turns the signals from the instrument into binary numbers—"bits" of data consisting of only 0 or 1—which the spacecraft transmits back to Earth for scientific analysis.

MARS LANDERS: WORKING ON THE SURFACE

MARS TRUE OR FALSE

TRUE

FALSE

MARS ORBITERS

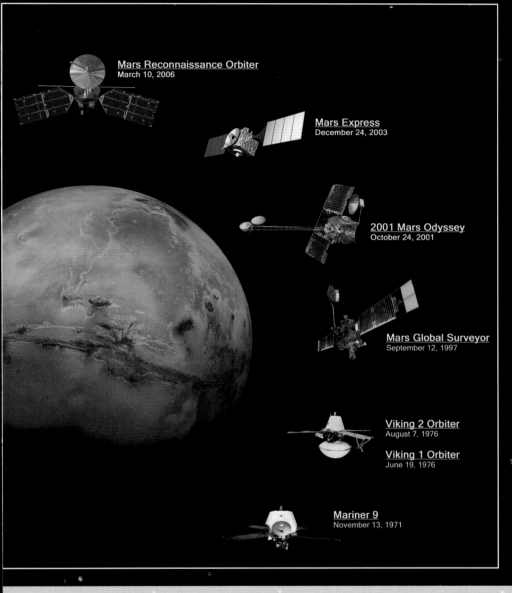

Mars Reconnaissance Orbiter
March 10, 2006

Mars Express
December 24, 2003

2001 Mars Odyssey
October 24, 2001

Mars Global Surveyor
September 12, 1997

Viking 2 Orbiter
August 7, 1976

Viking 1 Orbiter
June 19, 1976

Mariner 9
November 13, 1971

THE STORY CONTINUES

A future mission could land on the surface of Mars to pick up samples collected by a rover, blast off again, rendez-vous with another spacecraft waiting in orbit, and return the samples to Earth. New discoveries about Mars raise fresh questions and pose challenges for future explora-tion. Did the wet period on Mars allow life to develop, and if so how long did it survive? If humans choose to go to Mars, what are the resources and hazards that await them? What do the changes in climate on Mars teach us about our own plan-et, and about worlds around other stars?

MARS PATHFINDER

JUPITER

On March 2, 1972, Pioneer 10 was launched from the John F. Kennedy Space center to become the first space-craft to venture into the outer solar system. Eleven months later, the space-craft had successfully passed through the asteroid belt, and on December 3, 1973, came within 130,000 kilometers (80,800 miles) of the cloud tops of Jupiter.

Both Pioneer 10 and Pioneer 11, which encountered Jupiter a year later, had 11 scientific instruments and experiments designed to map magnetic fields and radiation in interplanetary space, and determine the atmospheric structure of Jupiter and Saturn. An additional magnetometer was added to Pioneer 11 to study high-strength magnetic fields.

Discoverer: Unknown
Spacecraft Encounter(s):
Pioneer 10 & 11 (1973, 1974)
Voyager 1 & 2 (1979)
Galileo (1995–2003)
Cassini - Huygens (2000–2001)

Mean distance from the Sun:
5.203 AU
(778,400,000 km/483,700,000 mi)
Length of Year: 11.86 years
Rotation Period: 9.92 hours
Mean Orbital Velocity: 13.06 km/s
(8.1 mi/s)
Inclination of Axis: 3.12°
Diameter: 142,980 km/88,846 mi
Number of observed satellites:
more than 60

MOONS

Jupiter has numerous moons, which make the Jovian system much like a miniature solar system. The four largest—Io, Europa, Ganymede and Callisto—were discovered by Galileo in 1610 and are known as the Galilean Satellites.

The other, smaller moons have their orbits either between Jupiter and Io, or outside the orbit of Callisto. The small outermost moons may be asteroids captured by the gravitational pull of Jupiter.

PLANET REVIEW

JUPITER

EARTH

MARS

MERCURY

VENUS

THE GALILEAN SATELLITES

IO

EUROPA

GANYMEDE

CALLISTO

NOISY JUPITER

Amount of Radio Noise

low

3km 300m 30m 3m 30cm 3cm 3mm

Wavelength

ATMOSPHERIC ROTATION

SATURN

In 1610, Galileo observed the peculiar appearance of Saturn, but was not able to recognize the true shape of the features on either side of the planet. It was not until almost 50 years later that the astronomer Christian Huygens discovered that the shapes were really rings. One obstacle to the recognition of Saturn's rings was that they are seen edgeon from Earth every 15 years, and thus seemed to disappear.

Discoverer: Unknown
Spacecraft Encounter(s):
Pioneer 11 (1979)
Voyager 1 & 2 (1980, 1981)
Cassini-Huygens (2004)
Mean distance from the Sun:
9.539 AU
1,427,000,000 km /886,700,000 mi
Length of Year: 29.46 Earth years
Rotation Period: 10.66 hours
Mean Orbital Velocity: 9.64 km/s
(6 mi/s)

Inclination of Axis: 26.73°
Diameter: 120,536 km (74,901 mi)
Number of observed satellites:
more than 25

Comparisons With Earth:
Diameter: 9.4 x Earth's
Average Distance from the Sun:
9.5 x Earth's
Mass: 95 x Earth's
Density: 0.13 x Earth's

THE VIEW FROM EARTH

Because Saturn's axis is inclined at 29 degrees, telescopic views change with different orbital positions of the Earth and Saturn. At times, the rings are seen edgewise from Earth and are nearly invisible.

GAPS IN THE RINGS

One of the mysteries of Saturn's rings is why they are confined to discrete zones separated by gaps such as the Cassini Division. One theory is that particles in these zones were gravitationally attracted by the moons of Saturn, and pulled into a new orbit. With the numerous moons and the possibility of additional smaller moons embedded within the rings, the gravitational interaction between the ring particles and Saturn's moons is quite complex.

ICY WORLDS

The six major icy satellites of Saturn have been known for many years through astronomical observations, although the Voyager encounters dramatically increased our knowledge of these bodies. All are composed of water ice with various amounts of silicate rock, and all have nearly circular orbits near the equatorial plane of Saturn.

MIMAS

ENCELADUS

TETHYS

DIONE

RHEA

IAPETUS

CLOUDS

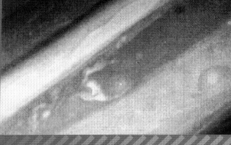

TITAN: A MOON WITH AN ATMOSPHERE

SATURN TRUE OR FALSE

TRUE

FALSE

URANUS

Discoverer: Sir William Herschel (1781)
Spacecraft Encounter(s): Voyager 2 (1986)
Mean distance from the Sun: 19.19 AU
(2.871 billion km/1.784 billion mi)

Length of Year: 84.01 Earth years
Rotation Period: 17.24 hours
Mean Orbital Velocity: 6.81 km/s (4.2 m/s)
Inclination of Axis: 97.92°
Diameter: 51,118 km (31,765 mi)

Number of observed satellites:
more than 20

Comparisons With Earth:
Diameter: 4.0 x Earth's
Average Distance from the Sun:
19.2 x Earth's
Mass: 14.5 x Earth's
Density: 0.22 x Earth's

URANUS AND ITS FIVE MAJOR MOONS

DISCOVERY OF URANUS' RINGS

On March 10, 1977, astronomers on board the Kuiper Airborne Observatory, a modified C-141 jet transport, discovered the rings of Uranus. While scientists were waiting for Uranus to occult (pass in front of) the star SAO 158687, they observed that the star's light dimmed repeatedly as the dark rings of Uranus passed between the star and the observatory.

NEPTUNE

NEPTUNE'S GREAT DARK SPOT

GAS
GIANT QUIZ

JUPITER

SATURN

URANUS

NEPTUNE

Discoverer: Galle, Challis, Adams, and Le Verrier (1846)

Spacecraft Encounter(s): Voyager 2
Mean distance from the Sun: 30.06 AU
(4.497 billion km/2.794 billion mi)
Length of Year: 165 years
Rotation Period: 16.11 hours
Mean Orbital Velocity: 5.43 km/s (3.3 mi/s)
Inclination of Axis: 29.6°
Diameter: 49,528 km/30,775 mi
Number of observed satellites: 8

Comparisons With Earth:
Diameter: 3.883 x Earth's
Average Distance from the Sun:
30.06 x Earth's
Mass: 17.14 x Earth's
Density: 0.31 x Earth's

THE OUTER LIMITS

A planet is defined by three properties:

* It is a celestial body that orbits the Sun.
* It is massive enough that its own gravity causes it to form in a spherical shape.
* It has cleared the neighborhood around its orbit.

Under this definition our solar system has eight planets: Mercury, Venus, Earth, Mars, Jupiter, Saturn, Uranus, and Neptune.

Because Pluto resides in an area of space populated by numerous other objects, it is no longer considered a planet. Pluto is now designated a dwarf planet, and it is the prototype of a class of objects located beyond the orbit of Neptune. Other dwarf planets are Ceres, the largest asteroid located between the orbits of Mars and Jupiter, and 2003 UB 313 which is an icy body that is larger and farther away than Pluto.

PLUTO

Discoverer: Clyde Tombaugh (January 23, 1930)
Spacecraft Encounter(s): New Horizons scheduled for July 2015
Mean distance from the Sun: 5.9 billion km (3.7 billion mi) / 39.5 AU
Length of Year: 248 years
Rotation Period: 6.4 days
Mean Orbital Velocity: 4.7 km/sec (3 mi/sec)
Inclination of Axis: 122.46 °

Diameter: 2,302 km (1,430 mi)
Number of observed satellites: 5

Comparisons With Earth:
Diameter: 0.18 x Earth
Average Distance from the Sun: 39.5 x Earth
Mass: 0.002 x Earth
Density: 0.36 x Earth

MOON REVIEW

GANYMEDE   CHARON

IO   TITAN   DEIMOS

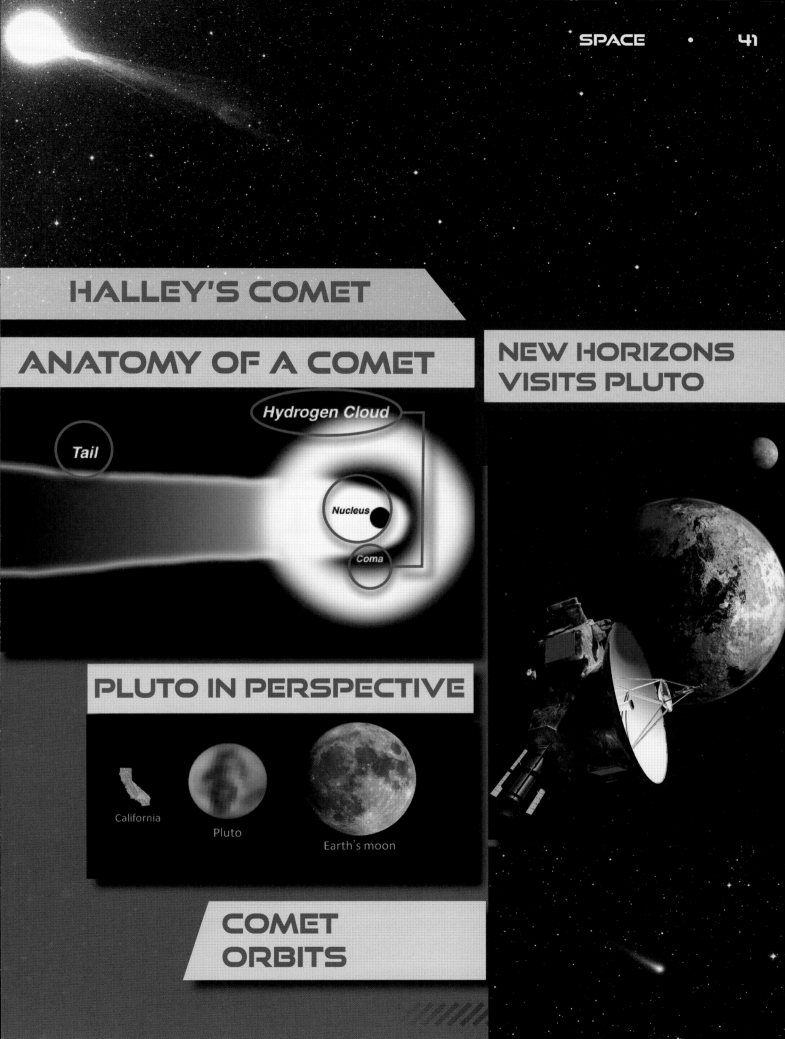

HALLEY'S COMET

ANATOMY OF A COMET

Hydrogen Cloud

Tail

Nucleus

Coma

NEW HORIZONS VISITS PLUTO

PLUTO IN PERSPECTIVE

California

Pluto

Earth's moon

COMET ORBITS

THE RACE TO SPACE

The Space Race grew out of the Cold War between the United States and the Soviet Union, the most powerful nations after World War II. For a half-century, the two superpowers competed for primacy in a global struggle pitting a democratic society against totalitarian communism.

Space was a crucial arena for this rivalry. Before a watchful world, each side sought to demonstrate its superiority through impressive feats in rocketry and spaceflight.

SOVIETS TAKE EARLY LEAD

1957: SPUTNIK

SPUTNIK 2

On October 4, 1957, a Soviet intercontinental ballistic missile (ICBM) launched Sputnik. This event startled the world, giving the impression that America was behind the Soviets in science and technology. Subsequent U.S. launch failures heightened that perception. The competition to build rockets now also became a competition to reach space.

STEP BY STEP

John Glenn, first American in orbit.

1958: EXPLORER 1

THE MOON ROCKET CHALLENGE

When the Space Race began, there was no rocket powerful enough to send a man to the Moon and back. Both the Americans and the Soviets had to develop a super-booster, or Moon rocket. The United States succeeded with the mighty Saturn V. The Soviets' N-1 Moon rocket never made it into space.

1959: LUNA 3

1961: FIRST MAN IN SPACE

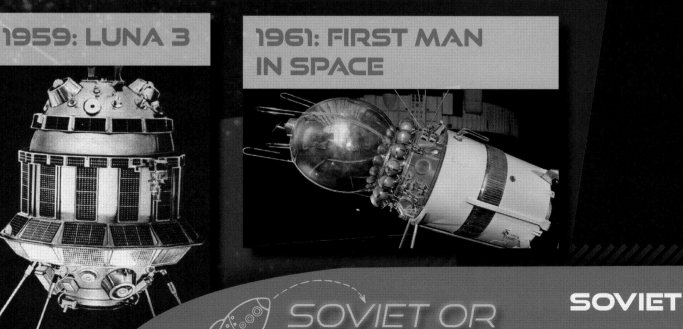

SOVIET OR AMERICAN?

SOVIET

AMERICAN

A PERMANENT PRESENCE

Before the race to the Moon ended, both the Americans and the Soviets were planning their separate futures in space. After the competitive short-term goals of manned spaceflight had been met in the 1960s, many advocates of space exploration envisioned a permanent human presence in space.

But support for manned missions to the Moon and beyond declined, and the focus for human activity in space shifted to near-Earth orbit. During the 1970s and 1980s, the United States and the Soviet Union took different approaches to manned spaceflight around Earth.

THE AMERICAN DIRECTION

THE SOVIET DIRECTION

SKYLAB: EARLY U.S. SPACE STATION

Lift-off of the Saturn V carrying Skylab on May 14, 1973.

A HOME AWAY FROM HOME

SOYUZ

The Soyuz spacecraft has three main components. The large spherical section at the front is the orbital module. The landing module is the bell-shaped section in the middle. The cylindrical section at the rear is the instrument module.

WORKING TOGETHER

GETTING UP THERE
TRUE OR FALSE

TRUE

FALSE

LIVING AND WORKING IN SPACE

Living in space for two weeks or for many months is both an adventure and an adjustment. On long missions the isolation from family, friends, and familiar surroundings can become a hardship. Shuttle astronauts were busy at least 16 hours a day working on a full schedule of mission tasks. On the Soviet and Russian space stations, cosmonauts have not been as heavily tasked.

SPACE SHUTTLE

Designed to operate on land, in the atmosphere, and in space, the Space Shuttle combined features of a rocket, an aircraft, and a glider. It could be launched, serve as a crew habitat and cargo carrier, maneuver about in orbit, return from space for an unpowered landing on a runway, and be ready to do it all again in a few weeks. The Space Shuttle's liquid-propellant main engines and turbopumps operated reliably at extremely high temperatures and pressures, mission after mission. Its main engines and solid rocket motors were the first ever designed for reuse.

PAYING FOR A RIDE

THE INTERNATIONAL SPACE STATION

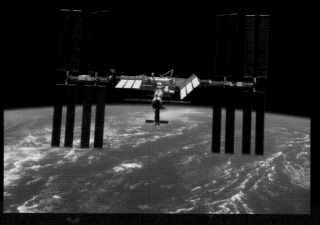

SHUTTLE-MIR MISSIONS

SPACE IS THE PLACE

A base in Earth orbit can serve many purposes:

* Biomedical research laboratory

* Microgravity research laboratory and materials processing facility

* Platform for astronomical and Earth-observing scientific instruments

* Training ground for long-duration spaceflight in preparation for human missions elsewhere in the solar system

* Way-station to the Moon or Mars

* Focus for advancing technology and maintaining spaceflight capabilities

A TOUCH OF HOME

CAN YOU DO THAT IN ORBIT?   YES   NO

THE SPACE SHUTTLE

To fulfill its variety of missions, the versatile Space Shuttle required crews with diverse skills and abilities, thus opening opportunities for scientists, engineers, women, and people of color to join a demographically diverse astronaut corps. The Space Shuttle democratized and internationalized human spaceflight. It enabled the growth of new disciplines in microgravity science—biological and physical sciences that explored the fundamental nature of anything in an environment without the dominant influence of gravity.

SHUTTLE MILESTONES

1983	1992
1984	1995
1990	

THE EVOLUTION OF A SPACECRAFT

During the early 1970s, various designs were proposed and rejected. NASA's concept in 1969 was a reusable manned booster and orbiter, but development costs were too high. In early 1972, NASA decided on a partially reusable space shuttle proposed by North American Rockwell. It included a reusable manned orbiter, two reusable solid-propellant booster rockets, an expendable fuel tank, and an enlarged cargo bay. President Richard Nixon approved the new space shuttle design.

SPACE SHUTTLE DISCOVERY

DISCOVERY MISSION ROSTER

8 communications satellite delivery flights
(1984–1989, 1995)

4 Department of Defense flights
(1985–1992)

9 flights with science labs, instruments, probes as primary payloads (1990–1998)

3 Hubble Space Telescope flights
(1990 deployment and 2 servicing visits, 1997, 1999)

2 flights to Russian space station Mir
(1995, 1998)

13 flights to the International Space Station
(1999–2011)

MISSION ACCOMPLISHED

MULTIPURPOSE CREW MEMBERS NEEDED

EXTRA-VEHICULAR ACTIVITY

Extra-vehicular activity, or EVA—working outside a spacecraft—changed the nature of human spaceflight. Technology and training made possible walking on the Moon, servicing the Hubble Space Telescope, and building the International Space Station. It remains crucial to our ongoing presence in space.

EVA requires a wearable spacecraft—the spacesuit—and specialized tools for astronauts to survive in the hazardous environment of space. Since the first spacewalks of Aleksei Leonov and Edward White in 1965, more than 200 astronauts and cosmonauts have amassed over 1,000 hours of EVA experience.

THE FIRST SPACEWALK

THE PERSONAL SPACECRAFT

INCREASED EVA COMPLEXITY

As spacecraft and their missions became more complex, so did EVAs. Performing EVA work from the payload bay of the nation's "space truck," Space Shuttle astronauts serviced satellites and tested methods later used in building the International Space Station.

Today, space station astronauts go outside to replace equipment, retrieve scientific experiments, and make repairs when damage occurs. They continue to require specialized tools and equipment to work efficiently.

MANIPULATOR FOOT RESTRAINT

DOUBLE UP

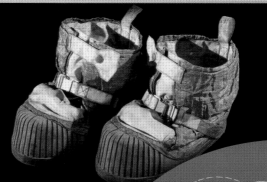

GENERAL PURPOSE TETHER

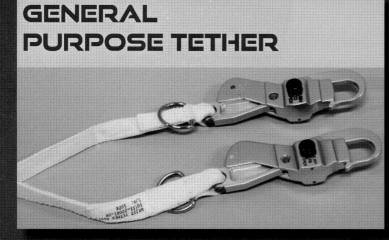

THE LAST LUNAR FOOTPRINTS

Tethers, handholds, and footholds are helpful in sports like rock climbing. They are really important in space. Without them the astronauts could float away from their spacecraft. If that happened, rescuing the astronaut would be almost impossible.

EVA
TRUE OR FALSE

TRUE

FALSE

VIEWING THE COSMOS

The Hubble Space Telescope is the largest astronomical telescope ever sent into space. It was launched in 1990. From its vantage point high above Earth's obscuring atmosphere, the telescope has provided astronomers with fascinating new information on the state of the universe. The Hubble Space Telescope was designed to be delivered into orbit by the Space Shuttle and to be serviced periodically in space by astronauts.

IMAGES FROM HUBBLE

PERFECT POSITION

SUBMILLIMETER ARRAY

HUBBLE CAPTURES DRAMATIC IMPACT

KEPLER THE PLANET HUNTER

OTHER OBSERVATORIES IN SPACE

Chandra X-ray Observatory: Launched and deployed by Space Shuttle *Columbia* on July 23, 1999. The telescope observes X-rays from high-energy regions of the universe, and, most significantly, is capable of imaging X-ray sources to a resolution not heretofore achieved.

Kepler Mission: Launched in 2009 by NASA in partnership with several organizations including the Smithsonian Astrophysical Observatory. It is designed to survey a portion of the Milky Way Galaxy to discover dozens of Earth-size planets in or near the habitable zone and determine how many of the billions of stars in our galaxy have such planets. Since March of 2009, Kepler has been continuously staring at more than 100,000 stars in a patch of sky in the constellation Cygnus.

FIRST VIEWS

CHRISTIAN HUYGENS

GALILEO GALILEI

SIR ISAAC NEWTON

EDWIN HUBBLE

CLYDE TOMBAUGH

ROCKETS AND MISSILES

The National Air and Space Museum's Rockets and Missiles collection includes launch vehicles and rocket engines from small thrusters to a gigantic F-1 motor from the Saturn V Moon rocket.

VANGUARD TV-2BU

ROCKET, LAUNCH VEHICLE, JUPITER-C, REPLICA, WITH EXPLORER 1 SATELLITE, REPLICA

ROCKET LINGO

PAYLOAD

THRUST

DRAG

ATTITUDE

STAGE

ROCKET MOTOR, SOLID FUEL, VANGUARD THIRD STAGE

ROCKET ENGINE, LIQUID FUEL, H-1

ROCKET ENGINE, LIQUID FUEL, APOLLO LUNAR MODULE ASCENT ENGINE

ROCKET, LIQUID FUEL, LAUNCH VEHICLE, SATURN V, WITH TRANSPORTER

ROCKET ENGINE, LIQUID FUEL, XLR-AJ-87-1, GEMINI BOOSTER, E TYPE

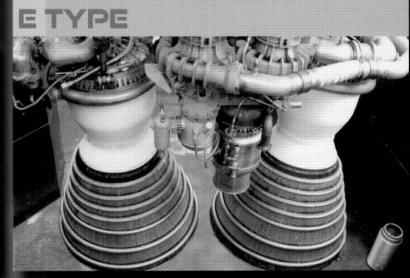

ROCKET MOTOR, LIQUID FUEL, APOLLO SERVICE MODULE REACTION CONTROL SYSTEM, POD

SPACE AGE ARTIFACTS

In 1966, President Lyndon Johnson signed a law that changed the name of the National Air Museum to the National Air and Space Museum to memorialize the development of both aviation and spaceflight. The Museum's collection on display expanded to include missiles and rockets.

The National Air and Space Museum collects many kinds of objects significant to the history of aviation and spaceflight. The collection, preservation, and interpretation of these objects is one of the primary ways we achieve our mission to "increase and diffuse knowledge."

G4-C PRESSURE SUIT, GEMINI 4

APOLLO 13 COMMAND MODULE

SLEEPING IN SPACE
TRUE OR FALSE

TRUE

FALSE

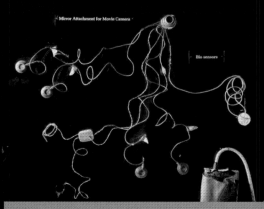

JOHN GLENN'S BIO-SENSORS, FRIENDSHIP 7

G-4-C HELMET, GEMINI 10

A7-L PRESSURE SUIT, APOLLO 11

LEFT GLOVE, MERCURY AURORA-7

APOLLO LUNAR SAMPLE RETURN CONTAINER, APOLLO 11

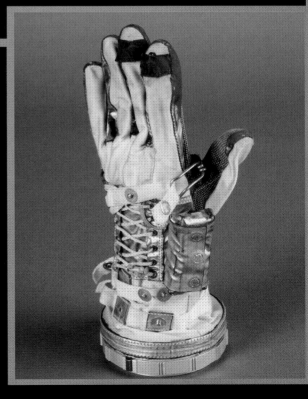

COSMIC CUISINE

Explorers and travelers throughout history have had to develop methods for preserving food and carrying enough food for their journeys. Space travel has demanded new methods of food preparation, preservation and packaging. Foods taken into space must be light-weight, compact, tasty and nutritious. They must also keep for long periods without refrigeration.

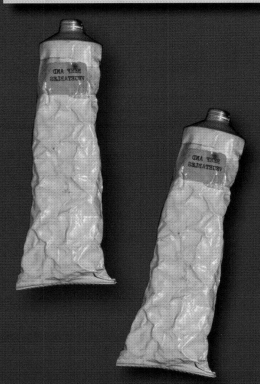

BEEF AND VEGETABLES, MERCURY, FRIENDSHIP 7

APOLLO 9 WATER DISPENSER

TEA WITH LEMON AND SUGAR, SHUTTLE

SAUSAGE PATTIES, APOLLO 11

APOLLO DRINKING DEVICE

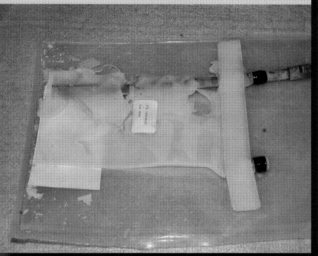

GREEN BEANS AND BROCCOLI, SHUTTLE, STS-1

FOOD TRAY, SHUTTLE

MEALS IN SPACE

APPLESAUCE

ICE CREAM

LETTUCE

TORTILLA

PEPPER

THAT'S ASTRONOMICAL

WHO WAS THE FIRST HUMAN IN SPACE?

JOHN GLENN

YURI GAGARIN

WHAT IS THE FIRST SPACE-CRAFT TO TRAVEL BEYOND OUR SOLAR SYSTEM?

PIONEER 10

VOSTOK 1

WHICH PLANET HAS TWO MOONS?

MARS

VENUS

WHICH PLANET IS CLOSEST IN SIZE TO THE EARTH?

MARS

VENUS

WHEN DID THE LAST APOLLO MISSION GO TO THE MOON?

1969

1972

AN ASTRONOMI-CAL UNIT (AU) IS THE DISTANCE BETWEEN THESE TWO BODIES.

EARTH AND THE SUN

EARTH AND THE MOON

WHO WAS THE FIRST AMERICAN TO WALK IN SPACE?

ED WHITE

ALAN SHEPARD

HOW BIG IS THE INTERNATIONAL SPACE STATION?

ABOUT THE SIZE OF A SCHOOL BUS.

ABOUT THE SIZE OF A FOOTBALL FIELD.

ABOUT HOW MANY STARS ARE IN THE MILKY WAY?

100 MILLION

100 BILLION